Girish Agarwal

Implementing a digital first sale doctrine

Comparative study of the E.U. and the U.S.A.

Anchor Compact

Agarwal, Girish: Implementing a digital first sale doctrine: Comparative study of the E.U. and the U.S.A., Hamburg, Anchor Academic Publishing 2015
Original title of the thesis: Resale of digital goods and copyright issues. Stance of the United States and the European Union

Buch-ISBN: 978-3-95489-348-5
PDF-eBook-ISBN: 978-3-95489-848-0
Druck/Herstellung: Anchor Academic Publishing, Hamburg, 2015

Bibliografische Information der Deutschen Nationalbibliothek:
Die Deutsche Nationalbibliothek verzeichnet diese Publikation in der Deutschen Nationalbibliografie; detaillierte bibliografische Daten sind im Internet über http://dnb.d-nb.de abrufbar

Bibliographical Information of the German National Library:
The German National Library lists this publication in the German National Bibliography. Detailed bibliographic data can be found at: http://dnb.d-nb.de

© Anchor Academic Publishing, ein Imprint der Diplomica® Verlag GmbH
http://www.diplom.de, Hamburg 2015
Printed in Germany

Table of contents

1   Introduction

To be honest, copyright law, regardless of the jurisdiction, is a complex piece of legislation. I find it difficult to comprehend many of the provisions and their purposes. And I am certainly not alone, there are many like me, even those who are well versed with its content find it baffling sometimes. So, then how can a lay man understand its myriad provisions without engaging a lawyer? Why he should have to engage one in the first place, aren't laws meant for lay men, then why only the experts understand them.

The answer lies in the way copyright legislation is drafted. The people who make laws cannot be expected to know the technicalities of the industries that have a stake in the legislation. Negotiations among stakeholders tend to produce laws that resolve interindustry disputes with detailed and specific statutory language, which rapidly grows obsolete.[1] So the law tends to be favourable to the interest holders, such as the publishers, and less inclined in serving the public interest.

"Otto von Bismark, the Iron Chancellor, warned that there are two artefacts as to which people are better off not knowing the production process; sausages and legislation".[2] If ordinary people are to grasp any sense and meaning out of the current copyright statutes then they need to be taught about its rules at an early stage. 'But our current copyright statutes couldn't be taught in elementary schools because students wouldn't understand it, their teachers wouldn't understand it; in fact copyright lawyers don't understand it'.[3] For them to understand, the law needs to be simple and short.

As a result "the inquiry relevant to copyright legislation long ago ceased to be, is this good bill? Rather the inquiry has been and continues to be, is this a bill that current stakeholders agree on?"[4]

1.1   Problem statement

It is not my intent to discuss what is copyright or it's drafting process, although, the basics relevant to this piece of work will be discussed. My focus will be on the doctrine of first sale as enshrined in the United States of America's (US) copyright law, and similarly, the right of exhaustion in the European Union (EU) directives. Traditionally, how this doctrine applies to

---

[1] Jessica Litman, Digital Copyright (Prometheus books, United States 2001) 63.
[2] David Nimmer, Copyright: Sacred text, Technology, and the DMCA (Kluwer Law International, Hague 2003) 497.
[3] Litman (n1) 72.
[4] ibid 63.

tangible products, such as a paper bound book, is not an issue, but when it comes to goods in the digital medium which are intangible in nature, such as an e-book, issues start to conjure up. This is due to the ephemeral nature of the fixation in the digital medium and the violation of one of the exclusive rights of the copyright owner, namely, the right of reproduction, when transferring a digital copy.

Thus, what are the obstacles in the way of transferring intangible goods, lawfully acquired, will be considered. It should also be kept in mind that developments in the US and the EU, with regard to the doctrines respectively, need not necessarily be the same. This polarity in the development will also be studied with reference to the relevant case laws.

1.2   Methodology

There has been much debate about the method of legal research. The most traditional method is the 'letter of the law' approach. This method consists of a positive analysis of the law, in other words, what the law is. It is unlike the normative approach wherein law is studied from the perspective of what ought to be and not what is. In here, I will adopt a positive analysis approach.

As this work concentrates on the doctrine of first sale/rule of exhaustion in the US and the EU, therefore, cases, articles and legal perspectives will largely be drawn from these jurisdictions. This work will use both, traditional legal sources like statutes and case laws, as well as academic works. There will, however, be references to international conventions and agreements such as the Berne Convention for the Protection of Literary and Artistic Works (as amended on September 28th, 1979), the WIPO Copyright Treaty of 1996 and the TRIPS agreement of 1994. As I will be studying two jurisdictions, a comparative analysis, wherever possible, will be undertaken.

1.3   Structure

I am going to divide this work into four components. The first part, I will call it 'the basics', which will give us a brief understanding of copyright relevant for the main discussion. This will include topics, such as, fixation of a work, reproduction and distribution rights of a copyright owner and what are digital goods.

The second part, which I will title 'the past', will deal with the development and the application of the doctrines in question. This will be necessary to fully understand the outcome of the application of the doctrines to digital goods. Topics, such as, the history and development of the first sale doctrine/rule of exhaustion and its justification will be studied.

The third portion of the work will be titled 'the present', which will be the main component. In here will be discussed the challenges associated with the reselling of digital goods. This will be done with the help of the Redigi and the UsedSoft cases from the US and EU, respectively. The trend towards licensing of digital goods instead of an outright sale by the copyright owners will also be discussed.

The fourth portion will rightfully be entitled 'the future' and as the name suggests will deal with unanticipated matters. Much of the writing and predictions will be my independent work with predictions based on the present situation.

2   The basics

2.1   Subject matter of copyright

According to Article 2 of the *WIPO Copyright Treaty, 1996, (WCT)*, copyright protects expressions and not ideas. So the manifestation of what is in your mind is necessary. In other words, the expression needs to be perceived by one of the senses, like reading a book, hearing a speech, listening to music or watching a movie. The *Berne Convention for the Protection of Literary and Artistic Works (BC)*, as amended in 1976, in Article 2, states that copyright shall extend to every production in the literary, scientific and artistic domain. This is rather a broad definition of what works are protected by copyright. Works will include books, journal and newspaper articles, poetry, song lyrics, computer programmes and other writings, dramatic and musical works, databases, paintings, drawings, sculptures, films, maps, and many more. ***Directive 2001/29/EC***, henceforth, the *Infosoc directive*, does not expressly address the issue of subject matter but it is addressed in Section 102(a) of the *US copyright act.*

2.2   Fixation of a work

Article 2(1) of the *BC,* says, that artistic and literary works are protected whatever may be the form of its expression. However, Article 2(2) of the *BC* gives the members of the union, the liberty to prescribe, that works in general or any specified categories of work, shall not be protected unless they have been fixed in some material form. The Spanish copyright law of 1987, in Article 10, specifies that the work shall be expressed in any manner whether tangible or intangible.[5] The Swiss law provides copyright protection irrespective of whether the work is fixed on a material medium or otherwise.[6] The EU directives do not mention fixation as a requirement for copyright protection.[7] In France for example, the *'Lacan case'*[8] provides that the work shall be protected in itself even if it has not been fixed in any material medium.[9] In this case, the court confirmed that oral presentation is protected in itself without the need for fixation. But, Section 102(a) of the *US copyright act* makes it mandatory that the work must be fixed in any tangible medium of expression...directly or with the aid of a device.

Fixation means expressing the idea in some material form. If I have poetry in mind which is not expressed in a material form, such as writing it on a piece of paper, it will be protected in many of the EU countries, technically, but it will not be protected in the US. This is because

---

[5] Estelle Derclaye, Research Handbook on the Future of EU Copyright (Edward Elgar, UK 2009) 140.
[6] ibid.
[7] ibid 139.
[8] T.G.I Paris, 11th December 1985, Dalloz 1987, somm. p. 155, note Colombet Claude.
[9] Derclaye (n5) 141.

fixation is not a requirement for copyright protection in many EU states, whereas, it is a requirement for copyright protection in the US.

Fixation basically serves the need to prove the existence of a work. It serves an evidentiary purpose.[10] So a certain amount of permanence is required. Owning a copy of Mario Puzo's 'The Godfather' means, either I could own a hard bound book (tangible good) which contains the author's ideas in print form or the work could be downloaded from the author's website (intangible good) in electronic form which is more contemporary.

But what if the author narrated the story, will that count as fixation? As the *BC* does not prescribe any mode or form of expression, in essence that speech will be protected. But narrating a story is of a transient nature and lacks permanence. This will make it difficult to prove the existence of the work in case of a copyright infringement claim.[11] However, if someone was to be writing down what the author was saying, and publishes it without his permission, it would amount to copyright infringement. Even if someone memorised what the author said and then later published it without the author's permission it would amount to infringement of his copyright.

2.3 Exclusive rights of a copyright owner

The rights necessary for understanding this piece of work is the reproduction right and the distribution right. There are other rights which a copyright owner enjoys but will not be touched upon.

2.3.1 Reproduction right

The reproduction right is basically the right to make copies of a work. It is one of the fundamental rights that a copyright owner enjoys. Article 9 of the *BC* contains the reproduction right. It grants it to authors of literary and artistic works. But it also permits the members of the union to allow reproductions in special circumstances, provided, that such reproductions do not conflict with the normal exploitation of the work and does not prejudice the legitimate interests of the author. This provision of the *BC* popularly known as the Berne three-step test has been applied in Article 5(5) of the *Infosoc directive* dealing with exceptions. The *WCT* does not address the reproduction right. But the agreed statements concerning Article 1(4) of the *WCT* states, 'the reproduction right as set out in Article 9 of the *BC* fully

---

[10] Douglas Lichtman, Copyright as a rule of evidence, 52 Duke L.J. 683, (2003).
[11] ibid.

apply in the digital environment.' Which means storing of copyright works in a digital electronic medium constitutes reproduction.

Article 2 of the *Infosoc directive* contains the reproduction right. It grants exclusive right to authorise or prohibit temporary or permanent reproductions, direct or indirect, by any means, for authors, for performers, for phonogram producers, for broadcasting organisations and for the producers of films. What is worth mentioning is that temporary acts of reproductions are also covered, which would at least in theory make copies in a random access memory (RAM) illegal. This would pose problems for intermediaries such as the Internet Service Providers who make temporary copies to enable transmission.[12] It will also pose problems for internet users as temporary copies are made all the time in the RAM.[13] But Article 5(1) of the *Infosoc directive* makes certain reproductions excusable which are temporary and an essential part of the technological process, such as transmissions in a network and a RAM copy. The reproduction has to be for a lawful use and should not be for any economic enrichment. Recital 33 of the *Infosoc directive* only goes on to confirm the position that temporary reproductions are allowed in certain cases, such as browsing and caching.

Directive 2009/24/EC, henceforth, the *computer programmes directive*, also provides that temporary and permanent reproductions or adaptation of a computer programme, necessary for a lawful users lawful use, is permitted.[14] However, according to Article 5(1) of the *computer programmes directive*, this is subject to contractual limitations, if any, set by the author of the computer programme. ***Directive 96/9/EC***, henceforth, the *database directive*, makes provisions for temporary reproduction which is necessary for access and use of the contents of the database, by a person who has a right to use that database.

In the US, reproduction rights are contained in Section 106(1) of the *US copyright act*. In *MAI Systems Corp. v. Peak Computer Inc.*[15], the question before the court was whether copies in a RAM implicates the reproduction rights. The court found that copying occurs when a computer programme is transferred from a permanent storage device to a RAM of a computer. However, Section 117 of the *US copyright act* makes exceptions to the reproduction right, making RAM copies permissible in the course of using a computer programme. But how far does this extend to other digital goods is questionable. On a lighter note, how permanent are

---

[12] Brigitte Lindner and Ted Shapiro, Copyright in the Information Society (Edward Elgar, UK 2011) 38.
[13] Ibid.
[14] Hector MacQueen, Charlotte Waelde, Graeme Laurie & Abbe Brown, Contemporary Intellectual Property (2nd, Oxford University Press, United States 2011) 178.
[15] 991 F.2d 511 (9th Cir. 1993).

copies in a RAM? It exists as long as there is power to the system. Once I switch off the power source the copies disappear.

There are other exceptions to the reproduction right which are covered under the fair use policy but will not be necessary to examine for the present discussion.

2.3.2 Distribution right

The right to distribute is a natural corollary to the right to reproduce. Through this right, the copyright owner is able to control the dissemination of his work to the public by sale, lease, rental or lending.

The *WCT* in Article 6 states that the copyright owner shall have the making available to the public right, of copyright work, through sale or other transfer of ownership. The agreed statements concerning Article 6 of the *WCT* makes it clear that it applies only to tangible copies. This in essence, is the right to distribute tangible copies of copyright work. Article 7 of the *WCT* which provides for the rental rights to the authors of computer programmes, cinematographic works and works embodied in phonograms, also applies to tangible copies only according to the agreed statements.

Article 8 of the *WCT* contains the right of communication to the public; it grants such a right to the authors of literary and artistic work and is meant for intangible goods which are transmitted over the internet. In addition to the communication to the public right it includes the right of 'making available to the public'. This has been a new edition in the *WCT*. The agreed statement concerning Article 8, states that a mere provision of physical facilities for enabling or making a communication, does not itself amount to communication. Physical by its very nature means something solid, something that you can touch and see. Communications to the public rights are also enumerated in the *BC* but in it they are not uniform. What the *WCT* did, it congregated the different communication rights under the *BC* and applied it to all literary and artistic works.

Article 3 of the *Infosoc directive*, which is similar to Article 8 of the *WCT*, mentions that the communication to the public right and making available to the public right in Article 3(1) of the *Infosoc directive*, will not be exhausted by any act of communication to the public or making available to the public. Article 4(1) of the *Infosoc directive* contains the distribution right for tangible goods. The *Infosoc directive* in Article 4(2) states, with respect to tangible goods the first sale or other transfer of ownership in the community by the right holder or with his consent shall exhaust his right to further control the distribution of that copy. These provisions of the *Infosoc directive* are in sharp contrast to Article 4(2) the *computer programmes directive*, wherein, it allows the exhaustion of not only a tangible copy of a computer programme but also an intangible copy of a programme, which has been distributed over the internet. This anomaly is due to because the *computer programmes directive* does not distinguish between tangible and intangible goods. It applies to instances where the computer programme has been downloaded from the authors website as well as when the programme has been bought embodied on a material medium such as a CD.

But the *database directive* makes a difference between tangible and intangible databases. Recital 33 of the *database directive* mentions that the question of the right of exhaustion does not arise in the case of online databases. This means that the exhaustion of right as enumerated in Article 5(c) of the *database directive* applies only to tangible copies.

It will be pertinent to note that the extinction of the right as mentioned in Article 4(2) of the *computer programmes directive*, Article 4(2) of the *Infosoc directive* and Article 5(c) of the *database directive*, applies only to first sale within the community. It does not apply to international sales.

It can get confusing to know what amounts to communication to the public and what amounts to making it available to the public. In the case of *Svensson v Retriever*[16], the Court of Justice of the European Union (CJEU) held that for an act of communication, it is sufficient that a work is made available to the public in such a way that the public may access it at a time and place individually chosen by them. This means they are one and the same thing or more precisely the making available to the public right is a sub category of the communication to the public right. In the US, in the case of *Capitol Records, Inc. v. Thomas*, the court came across this issue and held that making available to the public amounts to distribution in the online context.[17]

The significance of the different forms of dissemination lies in determining whether the rule of exhaustion is applicable to a particular transfer of ownership by sale or otherwise. Article 6(1) of the *WCT* contains the making available to the public right for tangible goods, and is used in the context of physical distribution. Then again in Article 8 of the *WCT*, the making available to the public right is mentioned alongside communication to the public right in

---

[16] Case C-466/12 [2014].
[17] 579 F. Supp. 2d 1210, 1225 (D. Minn. 2008).

relation to intangible goods, distributed by wire or wireless means. This means that the making available right is the right to distribute tangible as well as intangible goods.

In the *Infosoc directive*, in Article 3, making available to the public right is limited to intangible goods, unlike in the *WCT*. It does not extend to tangible goods. Article 4 of the *Infosoc directive* contains the distribution rights for tangible goods. But the *WCT* applies the making available to the public right to tangible and intangible goods. And the principle of exhaustion applies to the making available to the public right in Article 6(1) of the *WCT* but not to Article 8 of the *WCT*. If it was not for the agreed statements, it would be difficult to differentiate between the two making available to the public rights in the WCT. What the *WCT* should have done is used a different terminology instead of the making available to the public right in Article 6(1) to keep matters simple.

In the recent CJEU judgement in the *Svensson case* mentioned above, providing on a website a link to another website, where a copyright work is freely available, is not communication to the public within the meaning of Article 3(1) of the Infosoc directive. The link will constitute communication to the public only when the copyright work to which the links relate is access protected. This is because when the work is freely available there is no new public. The copyright owner targeted everyone, so the public who access the copyright work through the link, were taken into consideration by the copyright owner. The public have the option of accessing the work directly from the website where the work is freely available. So it makes no difference if they access the work through links on another website or directly from the website where the work is freely available.

The CJEU also opined that the provision of links to the work constituted making available to the public and used it synonymously with communication to the public right. Let us take an example of a website offering copyrighted goods. Users can download the materials directly from the website. By putting the goods on the website it amounts to making it available to the public (although an act of distribution has not taken place) and needs the copyright owner's permission, but is he communicating to the public? He is not transmitting the goods but only letting the public know that the goods are there. According to the reasoning in the *Svensson case,* it will also be communicating to the public as the making available to the public right is but a sub category of the communication to the public right. Supposing I download a song from the website, will my act of downloading still be communication to the public or will it be making it available to the public? In my view it will be distribution to the public and using the terminology communication to the public or making it available to the public for an act of download is misleading. But what I generally understand, after reading numerous literatures on the topic, is that communication to the public means transmission of digital goods, such as streaming movies and music, whereas, making it available to the public means transmissions, such as pay per view, on demand entertainment and it includes the act of downloading such digital goods. Thus the difference between the two is in the retention of the copy. If the buyer is able to keep a copy of the good then it will fall under making it available to the public otherwise it will be communication to the public.

The history of the making available to the public right shows, that it was crafted to cater to the music industry to protect it from piracy. So, instead of having to prove actual dissemination of the copyright work it was sufficient that the work was made available to the public, without actual dissemination. But then again you have to understand what is meant by distribution. Is it just making available copies of a copyright work or is it actual dissemination. What I think and what a prudent man would think is that distribution means when you give away copies of a copyright work and not just making it available.

As the extent of the different methods of dissemination of copyright work can vary depending on the copyright legislations of the individual countries, the CJEU in the *Svensson case* also concluded that Article 3(1) of the *Infosoc directive* cannot be interpreted more broadly to include wider range of activities than envisaged by the provision. In Sweden, for example, the copyright act offers an extended making available to the public right which includes communication to the public, public performance, distribution and display.[18]

In the US the right to distribute is contained in Section 106(3) of the *copyright act*. The limitation to this right is contained in Section 109, namely, the doctrine of first sale. Section 106(3) states that the copyright owner has the right to distribute copies or phonorecords of the copyrighted work. The US copyright act in Section 101 defines copies as material objects in which a work is fixed, other than phonorecords. Whereas, phonorecords is defined, in the same section, as material objects in which sounds, other than those accompanying a motion picture or other audio visual work are fixed. In both the instances it is a material object which are tangible goods. The question is how do these provisions apply to digital goods which are by their very nature intangible? Thus owner of a copy or phonorecord in Section 109 must mean owner of tangible goods. Therefore, it will be right to say that the first sale doctrine in the US does not apply to digital goods. To go even further, the copyright owner does not have

---

[18] Association littéraire et artistique international, Report on the making available and communication to the public in the internet environment, Available at : http://www.alai.org/assets/files/resolutions/making-available-right-report-opinion.pdf

the right to distribute digital goods. Even the making available right which was a new addition in the *WCT* is not explicitly expressed in the US copyright act.

2.4 Bits and bytes

Digital goods are basically information stored in bits and bytes.[19] They are transmitted over a network through wire or wireless means, more particularly the internet. The more accurate term for digital goods will be digital content and services.[20] Examples of digital goods will be e-books, online music, movies, databases, computer programmes, online newspapers, magazines and videogames and anything that can be digitized in ones and zeroes. Thus, any subject matter, eligible for copyright, that can be digitized and made available for consumption through digital technology are digital goods.

There are certain characteristics associated with digital goods, they are, namely: intangible, non-rival and non-excludable, able to proliferate and non-degradable.

The first characteristic, intangible, refers to the fact that digital goods are not perceptible to the sense of touch unlike tangible physical goods such as a paper bound book or a music cassette. Generally, intellectual property is intangible as long as it is unexpressed (an idea in the head), but becomes tangible when fixed in a material medium. At least that was the trend until now. But technological advances have revolutionised the medium and the manner in which copyright works are fixed. The thing with tangible goods is that the purchaser of a copy of a copyright work gets property rights in the medium in which the copyright work is fixed but that is not the case with intangible goods.

Supposing I buy a tangible copy of a book, I have paid for not only what is printed inside the book but also the paper which makes up the book. So in case I was able to erase everything written inside, I would still own the book. That book is my personal property, it is within my capacity to destroy it or alienate it. But the same cannot be said for intangible goods such as online music. For goods purchased online, I only pay for the copyright work and not the medium in which it is fixed because it is not fixed in any medium as such. Although I can delete the music which is akin to erasing, I don't have property rights the same way as I have in tangible goods.

---

[19] Claudia Loebbecke, Digital goods: An economic perspective, Encyclopedia of Information Systems, Volume 1, 635, (Elsevier Inc.) 2002.
[20] ibid.

The second characteristic, non-rival, refers to a good which can be enjoyed simultaneously by two or more persons without diminishing the utility of the good for the other person.[21] Non excludability refers to whether free riders can be excluded from enjoying the goods.[22] These characteristics are actually associated with public goods. As information is a public good according to economic analysis, we regard digital goods as information having the characteristics of public good.[23] Let us take an example of a public good such as a street light. It is non rival as the consumption by one person does not diminish the utility for another person. The light will shine for me as well as the hundredth passer-by. It is non excludable as you cannot legally exclude anyone from enjoying the benefits of the street light. Digital goods are non-rival in the sense that if I am browsing a website, another person can browse it too, without it being detrimental to me or him. A bar of chocolate will be a rival good because if one person consumes it the other persons share will diminish. Due to the nature of digital goods, like the ease with which it can be replicated and distributed, it is non excludable. Thus, copyright owners contend that if legal or technical means are not adopted to limit the number of free riders then the market for digital goods will diminish as they will become reluctant to release goods in the digital format.

The third characteristic of the ability to proliferate refers to the ease with which it can be copied and distributed.[24] Copies can be made effortlessly without any deterioration in quality unlike physical goods. It can also be distributed to countless people indifferent to geographical boundaries at lightning speed. To replicate and distribute physical copies requires a lot of resources. Digital goods also have the ubiquitous nature of being everywhere and at the same time they are nowhere.[25] That is not the case with physical goods.

The fourth characteristic non degradability means that they are indestructible.[26] Physical goods are subject to wear and tear but that is not the case with digital goods. The pages of a book will wear out but a digital copy of a book will last forever or until your hard drive gets corrupted.

---

[21] Niva Elkin-Koren and Eli M. Salzberger, Law, Economics and Cyberspace (Edward Elgar, UK 2004) 51.
[22] ibid 50.
[23] ibid.
[24] Danny Quah, Digital Goods and the New Economy (2002), Available at : http://econ.lse.ac.uk/staff/dquah/p/dp-0212hbne.pdf
[25] ibid.
[26] ibid (n19).

3 The past

3.1 Evolution of Copyright

In the days long gone, before the invention of the printing press, there was little need for copyright protection. Manuscripts were painstakingly written by hand. It included mostly of books and some documents. It must have taken months, sometimes even years to finish a work. Writing must not have been easy. The writing materials that I can think of haphazardly, are animal skin, cloth and wood. Paper must not have been used much as the demand for paper arose after the invention of the art of printing. The work produced would have been priced very highly and the only people able to afford it would have been noblemen. Therefore, literature was outside the grasp of ordinary people. In such a scenario, it can be inferred that copying a work would be unthinkable. Even if it were to be copied due to its intrinsic value, the cost and labour to reproduce it would make a person cautious before making a copy. Authors lacked any rights and had to be content with their paltry earnings.

All hail to Johannes Gutenberg for the invention of the printing press in the year 1448.[27] As a matter of fact, printing was already in existence in Eastern Asia although Gutenberg refined the technology.[28] Keeping the debate aside as to the origins of the printing press, it has been hailed as one of the most revolutionary technological advances of all times. It is because of it that so many of us enjoy literature and artistic work. Copies can be made at a fraction of time and cost. As with all technological advances, the sovereign is always wary about the harm that new technology poses. So it began to monopolise the printing business. Tis, birth of copyright law. The world's first national copyright law was the Statute of Anne passed in the year 1710 by the British Parliament.[29] I will take the chance here of mentioning that the US copyright law evolved based on the English law on copyright.[30] The authors for the very first time were given an opportunity to enrich themselves out of their intellectual creations. However, there is a gap of almost two and a half centuries after the printing press that the first copyright legislation came into being. That gap in time was necessary for the development of the legal concepts.[31]

Since the printing press, we have revolutionised technology even further. We are able to record sounds and pictures on mediums such as tape and compact disc. We are already in the

---

[27] Available at: http://web.mit.edu/invent/iow/gutenberg.html
[28] Available at: http://www.gutenberg.de/english/erfindu2.htm
[29] Arlene Bielefield and Lawrence Cheeseman, Technology and copyright law (Neal-Schuman Publishers, NY 1997) 4.
[30] ibid.
[31] ibid.

midst of the digital revolution and we are on the verge of moving towards the next technological revolution, whatever that might be. Copyright law has evolved to meet the problems of the digital era and will probably keep evolving to meet the challenges of new technology. This part is more worthy of discussion in the next section titled 'the present' so we will leave it for now.

3.2 Genesis of the first sale doctrine/rule of exhaustion

This is basically a limitation to the right to distribute.[32] We have already discussed what distribution rights are in relation to tangible as well as intangible goods. The doctrine was first codified in the *US copyright act of 1909*. What the doctrine basically states is that once a lawful copy of a copyright product is placed in the market, in other words, sold with the permission of the copyright owner, he exhausts his right to further distribute that particular copy. But that copy must be a lawful copy.

The doctrine was based on the English common law relating to the sale of real and personal property.[33] Its existence can be dated to the 1894 case of *Harrison v. Maynard, Merrill & Co.*[34] This case related to unbound leaves of books which were damaged by fire in a bindery. The bindery sold the leaves as waste. A second hand book seller later acquired those leaves, bound them up and sold them as books. The bindery brought an action against the second hand book seller to stop him from selling the books. The bindery's action failed. The doctrine was later affirmed in the 1908 case of *Bobbs-Merrill, Co. v. Straus.*[35] Bobbs-Merrill placed a notice on each copy of his book 'The Castaway' that it should not retail for less than a dollar. Macy and Company bought the books at wholesale for 40 percent less than the dollar and started retailing it for less than a dollar against the provisions of the notice. A suit was filed to restrain Macy from selling it for less than a dollar as the defendants were aware of the notice. But Bobbs-Merrill's case failed. The court held that copyright law does not create the right to limit the price at which works are sold by future purchasers who are not bound by contract or agreement.

In the EU the development is based on the need for an internal market and the free movement of goods and services. The origin of the exhaustion doctrine in the EU can be traced to the

---

[32] Victor F. Calaba, Quibbles 'n Bits: Making A Digital First Sale Doctrine Feasible, 9 Mich. Telecomm. Tech. L. Rev. 1 (2002), Available at : http://www.mttlr.org/volnine/calaba.pdf
[33] Bielefield (n29) 43.
[34] 61 F. 689 (C.C.A, Second Circuit 1894).
[35] 210 U.S. 339 ((Supreme Court 1908).

1971 case of *Deutsche Grammophon v. Metro*.[36] In this case Deutsche Grammophon sold the same records in Germany and France. But the French subsidiary sold the records at a lower price than that sold in Germany because of the market conditions prevailing in France. Metro bought the records in France and imported it to Germany for resale. The price at which Metro sold the records in Germany was below than what was charged by the authorised sellers in Germany. Deutsche Grammophon wanted to stop this practise. The court held that the rights in the record had been exhausted by putting the records in the market in France. As a result there can be no opposition to the importation by Metro. This case demonstrates the EU's concern for a single market and the free movement of goods and services.

As we have already discussed the various provisions of the right of exhaustion in the EU directives and the first sale doctrine in the US copyright law, I will not be undertaking such a task here.

3.3 The Justification for limiting distribution right

The purpose of copyright law is to progress literature and art. It does this by way of remunerating the people who produce such works.[37] In other words, monetary incentive acts like a reward for their talent and hard work. Once they have been sufficiently rewarded for their work, it makes little sense to allow them to control their work. So when a person purchases a copy of The Godfather, let's say for two hundred Kroner, that money or at least some of it, after the publisher has taken out his expenses, goes to the author as a reward for his work. Since he has been compensated for the copy there is little reason why he should control the further distribution of that copy. If you still give him distribution rights to that copy, it will be unfair to the buyer.

The second reason that I can think of will be to make the work available so that the society can benefit.[38] Libraries have been the guardian of literature for times immemorial. They have been lending to people who under normal circumstances will not be able to afford to buy a book. So with a nominal membership, members of the society can read from the vast collections that the library has to offer. And the library can only lend because of the first sale doctrine otherwise it would infringe the authors right to distribute.

---

[36] Case 78/70 [1971] ECR 487, [1971] CMLR 631.
[37] Ivy Choderker, The First Sale Doctrine defence as a limit on the right of publicity: Allison v. Vintage Sports Plaques, 19 Loy L.A. Entertainment L. Rev. 413, 422 (1999).
[38] Rachel Ann Geist, A License to Read: The Effect of e-books on Publishers, Libraries and the First Sale Doctrine, 52 Idea 63 (2012).

Another reason will be the acquisition of property rights.[39] As discussed, when a person purchases a copyright work fixed in a material medium, he owns the material medium. In other words he gets property rights in that medium. Together with other personal property rights he also acquires the right of alienation with respect to his personal property. So letting someone interfere with his right of alienation is not only unjust but bad law. As with physical copies digital works should also be accorded full property rights.

Did the legislators have secondary markets in mind?[40] Probably not, but this is one of the externalities of the doctrine. A big secondary market comes into existence in tangible goods because of it and sometimes even bigger than the primary market. This market adds to the prosperity of the economy, although, it could benefit the author as well, in ways such as making him popular among the masses thereby indirectly increasing the demand for his successive work. Does it benefit the buyer of an original copy of a work? Of course it does. Let's say I purchase a DVD knowing that I could sell it after getting bored of watching it, this adds value to my purchase. In this way I won't be hesitant in buying more products as I know that I will be able to dispose it off. My buying more products increases economic activity which in turn increases the demand for authors and artists. But some might argue that it kills the primary market. But that is not entirely true. What kill the primary market are illegal copies and not second hand copies. Primary markets still flourish in spite of the presence of secondary market. This is because new versions or editions that are available in the primary market, such as new editions of games or software, will not be available in the secondary market.

Lastly, the principle of exhaustion adds legal certainty to copyright law. In the absence of the principle there will be a need to negotiate new dealings with the copyright owner. Supposing I buy a tangible copyright product and imagine for a second that the rule of exhaustion did not exist. If I were to lend my tangible book to a friend I will need the copyright owners' permission for a lawful lending. Otherwise I will be infringing his distribution right. In other words, I will lack the power of alienation. The consequences of such a scenario will be disastrous as the complexity of the relevant rules allowing me to dispose of the copyright work after the first sale will be unfathomable.

---

[39] ibid (n37) 421.
[40] ibid 429.

4. The present

4.1 Crusade of technology

'The internet has been hailed as the most revolutionary social development since the printing presses'.[41] If I was writing this work in an era before the invention of personal computers, I would be using a pen and a paper, which to me suits more as I am old school. The speed at which technology has overtaken our lives today is astonishing. We have gadgets like tablets, smartphones, laptops, personal digital assistants and coupled with high internet speeds, thanks to optical fibres, it is like having a genie at your command. Information is available at your fingertips. The implications of this to the present discussion lies in the fact that copyright goods once enjoyed as a tangible medium has been turned into information stored in bits and bytes. Generally, if you ask me, it is a boon, this development in technology and computing power. One of the fundamental objectives of copyright law, which is to progress science and art, is achieved by facilitating access to knowledge. And what can be more convenient than the internet to achieve such an objective. Just to get an idea how advanced technology has become, the computers that put man on the moon is trivial compared to the technology that is put in today's ordinary smart phones.

But from the point of view of the copyright owners, this advancement in technology is a bane. According to them, the internet is one big gigantic copying machine. The reproductions are perfect without any deterioration in quality. The illegal copy can also be shared around the world at the click of a mouse. So naturally their guards are on. But that is not entirely true. Technology has also at the same time allowed the copyright owners to gain more control of their work through technological protection measures, which restrict transferability of digital goods as they are locked up. If a CD is region coded, even if I exercise my right to resell, it hardly makes a point as it can be played only on selected devices limited to geographical locations.

4.2 Issues in the resale of digital goods

Basically, the issue in reselling digital goods is that it necessarily involves making a copy. Reproduction is an unavoidable technological process in transferring digital goods. The copy implicates the reproduction rights of the copyright owner. That is why the doctrine of first sale/rule of exhaustion is inapplicable to digital goods. I will address the issues relating to the

---

[41] Litman (n1) 12.

resale of digital goods with the help of the EU case of *Oracle v. UsedSoft*[42], henceforth, the UsedSoft case, and the US case of *Capitol Records, LLC v. Redigi Inc.*[43], henceforth, the Redigi case, which go on to establish their respective stances, well at least for now.

Other issue that will be discussed is the licensing of digital goods as it restricts after sales rights.

4.2.1 The UsedSoft case

To begin with, I will mention, that the UsedSoft case, is a software licensing case, and its ramifications to other digital goods is sceptical. The issue of its outcome to other digital goods was not addressed by the Court of Justice of the European Union (CJEU). But as the problems associated with the resale of software can be said to be congruent with the resale of other digital goods, a comparison is not totally farfetched. The UsedSoft case will be discussed in light of the *WCT, Infosoc directive* and the *computer programmes directive.*

The facts of the case in question can be summarised as follows,

Oracle International Corp., henceforth Oracle, develops and markets computer software. It distributes 85% of its software by online means, i.e. by making it available for download to its users from its server. The download is free but to use the software Oracle offers group licences for a minimum of 25 users each. Thus in order to use the software the user needs to enter into a license agreement with Oracle, each licence agreement for a minimum of 25 users each. In addition a maintenance agreement could also be entered between the user and Oracle which updates the software but which is not necessary to use the software. The maintenance agreement can be cancelled at any time by the user. The user licence agreement reads as below,

"With the payment for services you receive, exclusively for your internal business purposes, for an unlimited period a non-exclusive and non-transferable user right free of charge for everything that Oracle develops and makes available to you on the basis of this agreement."

UsedSoft markets used software licences including those of Oracle. It acquires those licences or parts of them when the licence relates to a greater number of users than required by the original licence holder, directly from Oracle's customers. Particularly in October 2005, UsedSoft offered for sale Oracle licences in issue stating that they were current in the sense

---

[42] C-128/11 [2012] 3 C.M.L.R. 44.
[43] 934 F.Supp.2d 640 (S.D.N.Y. 2013).

that the maintenance agreement between the original licence holder and Oracle was still in force. Customers of UsedSoft not in possession of the Oracle software were to download the software directly from Oracle's server and those in possession of the software but who were in need of extra licences for extra users were to copy the software from their internal servers into the memory of their workstations of the extra users.

Oracle contended that as the transfer of its software to its customers was not a sale and that the non-exclusive and non-transferable licence only gave a right to use the software, it did not exhaust its distribution right to the copy of the software. Moreover, it was communication to the public within the meaning of Article 3(1) of the Infosoc directive as the software was downloaded online and was not distributed on a tangible medium; therefore, exhaustion does not apply in this particular case. Thus, UsedSoft infringed its copyright by selling used licences of its software.

Legal provisions

The provisions of the *WCT* that are relevant for an analysis are, Article 6(1) which contains the making available to the public right for tangible copies of work through sale or other transfer of ownership, Article 6(2) which allows the contracting parties to determine the conditions for the exhaustion of the making available to the public right with respect to tangible copies, Article 7(1)(i) which contains the author's right of rental with respect to computer programmes and Article 8 which contains the communication to the public right and making available to the public right, of works, distributed by wire or wireless means. Article 6 is relevant as it explicitly states that the exhaustion of right after the first sale should apply to tangible copies, Article 7(1)(i) is relevant as it states that the exhaustion of right does not apply to computer programmes disseminated by way of rental and Article 8 is relevant as it tells us that the exhaustion of right does not arise in the case of online distribution of digital goods.

The following provisions of the *Infosoc directive* are relevant for an analysis. Article 1(2) (a) accords special status to the *computer programmes directive*. This Article is important in order to determine whether the provisions of the *Infosoc directive* can be applied to the *computer programmes directive*. Article 2 gives exclusive right to the copyright owner, in this case the author, to reproduce his work temporarily or permanently by any means. As the only person entitled to reproduce a work is the copyright owner himself, a transfer of digital goods including software by anyone other than the copyright owner will implicate the reproduction rights of the author, as every transfer in the digital medium necessarily involves making a copy. Article 3(1) gives authors the exclusive right to communicate the work to the public and make the work available to the public by wire or wireless means and Article 3(3) states that the communication to the public and making available to the public rights are not exhausted. This is relevant because if a transfer by sale or other transfer of ownership of digital goods including software is considered as communication to the public or making available to the public then the rule of exhaustion does not apply. Article 4(1) gives to authors the right to distribute tangible copies of their work to the public by sale or other transfer of ownership and Article 4(2) states that the distribution rights for tangible copies are exhausted upon the first sale of a copy within the community, by the right holders consent. Article 4 is relevant because if distribution right is meant only for tangible copies of copyright work then a sale or other transfer of ownership of digital goods including software is not distribution within the meaning of the *Infosoc directive* and the rule of exhaustion of right is limited to tangible copies of copyright goods. In Article 5, the relevant provisions are 5(1) (b) which permits acts of reproduction which are an essential and integral part of the technological process and whose sole purpose is to enable a lawful use with no economic significance and 5(2) (b) which permits acts of reproduction on any medium for private use by a natural person and which have no commercial value. These provisions are important as the implication of the reproduction right in the transfer of digital goods including software can be negated by relying on these exceptions.

The following provisions of the *computer programmes directive* are relevant. Article 4(1) (a) which contains the right of reproduction and which allows the author of the computer programme to authorise the permanent or temporary reproductions of the computer programme by any means. This provision is relevant as it states that reproduction of a computer programme without the author's authorisation is infringement of his reproduction rights. Article 4(1) (c) contains the author's distribution right and allows the author to disseminate his work to the public in any form. This will include distribution of software on a CD-ROM as well as by computer downloads. Article 4(2), however, states that the distribution rights of the author of a computer programme shall be exhausted, upon the first sale in the community, of a copy of a computer programme, with the right holders consent except for the rental rights. Lastly, Article 5(1) which states that in the absence of any contractual provisions, temporary and permanent reproductions of a computer programme within the meaning of Article 4(1) (a), shall be permissible by a lawful acquirer where they are necessary for the use of the computer programme.

Questions of law

There were three questions referred to the CJEU by the Federal Court of Justice in Germany, where the case was in appeal from the Regional Court. The questions were (a) whether the right to distribute an intangible copy of a computer programme exhausted in accordance with Article 4(2) of the *computer programmes directive*, if the lawful acquirer had made a copy with the right holders consent by downloading the computer programme from the internet, (b) whether a person who can rely on the exhaustion of right to distribute a copy of a computer programme, a lawful acquirer within the meaning of Article 5(1) of the *computer programmes directive* and (c) whether a person who had acquired a used software licence to generate a programme copy also rely on the rule of exhaustion within the meaning of Article 4(2) of the *computer programmes directive*, if the first acquirer had erased his copy of the programme.

The issues in all the three questions can be settled by answering just the first question. If the right to distribute an intangible copy of a computer programme is exhausted within the meaning of Article 4(2) of the *computer programmes directive* then the person relying on the exhaustion of right is a lawful acquirer within the meaning of Article 5(1) of the *computer programmes directive*. Therefore any person acquiring the software from a lawful acquirer within the meaning of Article 5(1) of the *computer programmes directive* can also rely on the rule of exhaustion within the meaning of Article 4(2) of the *computer programmes directive*. If the answer to the first question is in the negative then the answer to the other two questions will also be in the negative.

In brief, I will sum up the important findings of the CJEU in this case. The court found that the basic properties of the licence had to be taken into consideration. So long as it contained the basic properties of a sale, such as a onetime fee and not limited in time, it was a sale. It made no difference if the programme was distributed embodied in a material medium such as a CD-ROM or by the means of downloading. Therefore, the right to distribute was exhausted in accordance with Article 4(2) of the *computer programmes directive*. It also stated that Article 3 and 4 of the *Infosoc directive* had to be interpreted in light of Article 6 of the *WCT*. This has been held in para H13 of the judgement. Over here the CJEU erred as Article 3 of the *Infosoc directive* deals with intangible goods transmitted by wire or wireless means, it can only be interpreted in accordance with Article 8 of the *WCT* and cannot be interpreted in accordance with Article 6 of the *WCT*, which according to the agreed statements deals with tangible copies of goods. But Article 4 of the *Infosoc directive* can be interpreted in accordance with Article 6 of the *WCT* as both deals with tangible goods. It also stated that the licence could not be divided and sold for individual users. The original acquirer must also make his own copy of the programme unusable at the time of reselling the licences in order not to infringe the reproduction right of the right holder.

Analysis

I will analyse this case separately against the *WCT, Infosoc directive* and the *computer programmes directive* without overlapping the provisions of the instruments. I will discuss it in my own manner but keeping the soul of the judgement. Let us consider whether the transfer of software form Oracle to its customers was a sale or a licence. The software can be downloaded by anyone for free. The only problem being that the software is locked, in other words, it is unusable unless I enter into a licence agreement on the payment of a onetime fee. The licence makes it very clear that I can use the software till perpetuity. But it also specifies that it is non-transferable. It cannot be classified as rental as rental implies for a limited period in time according to Recital 12 of the *computer programmes directive.* I won't be wrong if I said that the transfer of software is essentially a sale since it involves only a onetime fee and the right to use it till perpetuity, the basic characteristics of a sale, but disguised in the form of a licence. The *WCT* makes it very clear that Article 6, which contains the right of making available to the public, applies only to tangible copies. So the transfer of software does not fall within Article 6 of the *WCT* as Oracle transferred an intangible copy of the software to its customers. Article 7 of the *WCT* applies to rental which is outside the scope, as rental implies for a limited period in time and the transfer of the software from Oracle to its customers was for an unlimited period in time. Article 8 of *WCT*, which contains the communication to the public right and making available to the public right can be applied as Oracle transferred the software to its customers by allowing them to download the software from its website, internet transmissions will be communication to the public. Therefore, Oracle made available to the public the software in a manner that it could be accessible by the public from a place and at a time individually chosen by them. As there is no exhaustion of communication right in terms of Article 8 of the *WCT*, even if it is a sale, UsedSoft infringed Oracle's copyright by reselling its software or the rights thereto without its permission.

The results should be the same if the problem was cast against the *Infosoc directive* as it implemented the provisions of the *WCT.* Recital 28 states that the distribution right and its exhaustion apply only to tangible copies. Recital 29 states that the exhaustion of right does not apply to services including online services. To understand what is meant by online services it is best to understand the difference between goods and services in the physical world. When you pay a lawyer or a doctor you are paying for his services. He does not sell you any goods. It is easy to classify between goods and services in the physical world. But in the online context the line between selling goods and services is blurry. Some examples of an online service are an Email service and internet banking services provided by banks. The internet itself can be classified as an online service. So selling software online will be selling a good and not a service although the act of updating and maintaining the software will fall under online services. Accordingly, only the maintenance agreement of the Oracle software, in the sale of the software can be classified as an online service which was not integral to use Oracle's software. So the transaction is not an online service. It was the transfer of ownership of the software. When we talk about exhaustion of right it means exhaustion of distribution right as reproduction rights are not exhausted. However reproduction rights are subject to certain exceptions such as under Article 5(1) (b), temporary reproductions for a lawful use of a work.

Article 3(1) of the *Infosoc directive* has been implemented in line with Article 8 of the *WCT*. It contains the communication to the public and making available to the public right. Therefore, the transfer of software from Oracle to its customers will fall within Article 3(1) of the Infosoc directive and Article 3(3) of the same directive mentions that the right in Article 3(1) shall not be exhausted. Article 4 of the *Infosoc directive* which contains the distribution right is meant only for tangible goods. Thus, as the transfer of the software from Oracle to its customers was done electronically by download (intangible copy) the provisions of Article 4 do not apply. Hence, the original acquirer of the software did not have the rights to resell it to UsedSoft who in turn did not have the right to resell it to its customers as Oracle never exhausted its communication to the public or making available to the public right. By transferring the software the original acquirer as well as UsedSoft infringed the reproduction right as enshrined in Article 2 of the *Infosoc directive* as well as the communication to the public and making available to the public right as enshrined in Article 3(1) of the *Infosoc directive*. As it was an unlawful use of the software the original acquirer or UsedSoft cannot avail themselves of the exceptions to the reproduction rights mentioned in Article 5(1) (b) or 5(2) (b).

Now let's discuss the problem against the backdrop of the *computer programmes directive*. Will the outcome be the same? Article 1(2) (a) of the *Infosoc directive* states that in no way does it affect the provisions of the *computer programmes directive*. This means that the *computer programmes directive* is a special legislation exclusively for computer programmes and is not overridden by the provisions of the *Infosoc directive*. Recital 7 of the *computer programmes directive* clearly states that computer programmes shall include programmes in any form including those that have been fixed into hardware. Therefore, it will include intangible copies as well, such as the ones downloaded from the internet. Article 4(2) of the *computer programmes directive* states; the first sale of a copy of a programme with the right holders consent shall exhaust the distribution right within the community. Copy in this context has to be understood as meaning any copy, including intangible copies. If the intention of the legislature was to limit the provision to tangible copies only, in my view, it would have been explicit about it. As ninety percent of the software that is consumed is distributed online by download, if the provisions of Article 4(2) was to apply only to tangible copies the provision is as good as dead. This reasoning also follows from recital 7 of the *computer programmes directive* and it cannot be interpreted as meaning only tangible copies. As the transfer of the software from Oracle to its customers was a sale, it does come within Article 4(2) as there is no communication to the public or making available to the public right in the *computer programmes directive*. Nor can it be inferred from the *Infosoc directive*. As such, the original acquirer has the right to resell the programme which in essence is his right to use the programme. In this case there can be no infringement of the reproduction rights, although according to Article 4(1) (b) it is only the right holder who can authorise the temporary and permanent reproduction. This is because Article 5(1) allows a lawful acquirer of a computer programme to reproduce the programme for the use of the computer programme. UsedSoft by selling used software licences of Oracle does not infringe Oracle's copyright.

With regards to UsedSoft not infringing the reproduction rights of Oracle I beg to differ slightly from what the CJEU discussed. CJEU concluded that UsedSoft was a lawful acquirer within the meaning of Article 5(1) of the *computer programmes directive* and thus was authorised to reproduce the programme for use. Lawful acquirer means a person who has acquired the software lawfully, whether through sale, rental, hire or otherwise. What I noticed in the case law was that there was no transfer of software from the original acquirer to UsedSoft or from UsedSoft to its customers. The only thing being transferred was the user licence. Therefore, the infringement of reproduction rights did not arise. Persons who did not own the software were to download the software directly from Oracle's website which was free for everyone to download. Even if that is termed as reproduction it is with the right holders consent. Essentially the copy that was used by the original acquirer and UsedSoft customers were individual copies. The original acquirer did not load the software onto

30

UsedSoft's website nor did UsedSoft make it available for download to its customers from its website.

Browsing through Susensoftware's website which sells used software's, just like UsedSoft, there is a page in where it tells you how to transfer used software.[44] Supposing I buy a used software from the website, the only thing that is delivered to me are documents of a valid sale and title, such as, a purchase and maintenance contract, general terms and conditions of the manufacturers contract, last invoice of maintenance, confirmation of deletion of the original acquirers copy, purchase contract between the supplier (original acquirer) and Susensoftware and letter from the manufacturer of the software that the licence has been transferred to you. But there is neither a transfer of the copy of the software from the original acquirer to Susensoftware nor a transfer from Susensoftware to its customers. Only a transfer of licence takes place which is later confirmed by the manufacturer of the software. Customers of Susensoftware have to download the software from the manufacturer's website or they are supplied a CD-ROM containing the software once they have paid for the used software licences and received the documents confirming a valid sale and title.

The only time reproduction was taking place in the UsedSoft case was when an original acquirer who was in possession of the software decided to buy extra licences. Then the software was transferred from the internal server of the original acquirer to the work stations of the extra users. As the CJEU held that the licence had to be sold as a whole, it could not be divided for individual users. As selling individual licences was illegal so was reproducing the software on extra users workstations.

For a moment I will assume that the software itself was being transferred. As every transfer in the digital environment entails a temporary and permanent reproduction of that copy it would mean that the right holder's reproduction right would be infringed. According to Article 5 of the *Infosoc directive*, reproductions can only be allowed for exceptional cases. The list is exhaustive. Reselling used intangible software or any other digital good will run afoul of the provisions of the *Infosoc directive's* right of reproduction. As transferring an illegal copy is not a lawful use within the meaning of Article 5(1) (b) it would implicate the reproduction rights of the right holder. It is because of Article 5(1) (b) that I am able to browse the internet and make temporary copies in the RAM of my computer. Otherwise I would be infringing the copyright owners' right of reproduction, as temporary reproductions are an unavoidable part

---

[44] Available at : http://www.susensoftware.com/used-licenses/sap/

of the technological process of using computers. Thus, the rule of exhaustion is limited to distribution of tangible goods. Therefore, resale of digital goods cannot be accommodated within the *Infosoc directive*.

On the other hand Article 5(1) of the *computer programmes directive* also allows acts of reproduction by a lawful acquirer for the use of the programme, in the absence of any contractual provisions to the contrary. In the UsedSoft case how far will it be correct to say that UsedSoft, having lawfully purchased used software licences from the original acquirer, is a lawful acquirer within the meaning of Article 5(1) of the *computer programmes directive* is debatable? On a deep reading of the Article 5(1) of the *computer programmes directive,* it tells us that the provision is intended for after sale reproductions. This means that reproduction is permissible only after a person has legally acquired the software and not before that. If selling a used software licence amounts to selling the software itself then UsedSoft is a lawful acquirer within the meaning of Article 5(1) of the *computer programmes directive* and has a right to permanently reproduce the computer programme for personal use. If not, it will be infringing Oracle's reproduction right. But even then, if the transfer of the software is not a sale and the contractual provisions limit the rights granted by Article 5(1) of the *computer programmes directive*, the lawful acquirer, in this case UsedSoft will not have the right to reproduce the programme. If the licence granted by Oracle was limited in time or required recurring fees the outcome of the case would be entirely different as the rule of exhaustion to computer programmes applies only to sale according to the *computer programmes directive*. But the term sale has to be interpreted broadly.

Having examined the issues relating to the case it is time now to examine the conundrum and its effect to other digital products. If you try and interpret the *computer programmes directive* in light of the *Infosoc directive* or vice versa it's going to be a disaster. This is because the *Infosoc directive* classifies copyright works as tangible and intangible. For intangible goods in accordance with Article 3 of the *Infosoc directive*, the copyright owner has the right of communication to the public and the making available to the public right. For tangible goods the copyright owner has the right of distribution in accordance with Article 4 of the *Infosoc directive*. The *Infosoc directive* applies the rule of exhaustion only to tangible goods.

On the other hand, the *computer programmes directive* in accordance with Article 4(2), does not make any such classification. It applies the rule of exhaustion to tangible as well as intangible goods, provided the transfer of the software is a sale.

The provisions relating to distribution and the exhaustion of rights are dissimilar in both the directives (*Infosoc directive* and the *computer programmes directive*). If the case in question was decided solely according to the *Infosoc directive* the outcome would have been in favour of Oracle. This is because the transfer of the software from Oracle to its customers would have fallen under the communication to the public right for which there is no rule of exhaustion. The only solution is not to mix the two directives and keep the *Infosoc directive* exclusively for other digital products, with the exception of computer programmes and databases, for smooth application.

But why have special provisions for computer programmes and databases? In the end they are bits and bytes just like other digital goods. Other digital content should be accorded the same liberty to take advantage of the rule of exhaustion and allow reproductions like in the case of computer programmes. If it does not matter if computer programmes are made available on CD-ROMs or by internet downloads it should not matter for other digital goods as well.

4.2.2 The Redigi case

The US district court case of Redigi is a fine example of the issues involved with reselling other digital goods. In going about this case, I will restrict my analysis to the provisions of the *US copyright act*. The brief facts of the case are as follows.

Capitol Records LLC is the copyright owner of much music sold on Redigi's website. Redigi Inc. is a technology company and operates a website where users can sell their legally acquired music files and buy used digital music from others, who have sold their music. It is like visiting a second hand record store. Redigi's media manager scans the user's computer and analyses files eligible for sale. Only music that has been purchased from Apple's iTunes or from another Redigi user is eligible for sale. Music burned from CDs or downloaded from file sharing websites are ineligible. Media manager continually runs on the user's computer to make sure that the sold file is not retained. But it cannot detect copies stored in other locations. If a user in spite of selling a file keeps a copy on his computer his account with Redigi is suspended. The music once sold is uploaded to Redigi's server. Redigi asserts that the process of transferring the file involve migrating a user's file packet by packet, so that the data does not exist at two places at the same time. Capital asserts it necessarily involves copying.

After a second analysis, that the file has not been tampered with the uploaded file is stored in Redigi's server. The buyer can download the file to his computer or other devices or stream it from the server when necessary. If the buyer sells his file his access is terminated and assigned to the new user. No money changes hands in these transactions. Instead user's buy music with credits. Credits are either purchased or acquired from other sales. The credits cannot be exchanged for money. To preview the music before buying it Redigi entered into a licensing agreement with third parties. It sends its user's to iTunes or YouTube to preview. Redigi earns a fee for every transaction. When user's purchase a file 20% of the sales price is allocated to the seller, 20% goes to an escrow fund for the artist and 60% is retained by Redigi.

The court determined that Redigi infringed Capitol's reproduction and distribution right as every transfer in the digital medium necessitated the creation of a new copy. We will take the issues one at a time.

Analysis

As mentioned, reproduction rights are contained in Section 106(1) of the *US copyright act*. It states that the copyright owner has the right to reproduce the copyrighted work in copies or phonorecords. Copies or phonorecords are material objects as defined in Section 101 of the *US copyright act*. Buying music online is entirely different from buying a phonorecord. There is no material medium provided by the copyright owner, only the copyrighted work. Instead it uses the buyer's material medium such as a hard drive where the songs are stored. When purchasing songs online, or any other digital goods for that matter, the song will be at many places at the same time. So when Redigi's user's purchase songs from Apple's iTunes, when downloading the song to their computer the song is present in Apple's server, at the same time it is travelling in packets through the internet network and when it reaches the computer the code is embedded in the hard drive. With tangible goods once a copy is given away you are short of one copy. But the song on Apple's server does not have to be replaced by a new song. The same song can be downloaded again by another user which saves a lot of money to the copyright owner as the the marginal cost of producing the additional unit of the product is nil. But then again it can be argued that the cost involved in producing the first unit is exceptionally high. In order to gain back the cost, it is necessary for the copyright owners to charge for every digital copy that is sold to the customers. If this was not the case there would be no incentive to produce copyright works in the digital medium.

Redigi's media manager analyses goods eligible for upload. Only songs that have been purchased on iTunes are eligible for upload. In the first instance there is a valid sale between iTunes and the user. The court determines that in order to transfer the song, you have to transfer the hard drive where the song is stored as uploading involves a reproduction on Redigi's server. As the hard drive cannot be transferred through the network there can be no first sale defence to distribution of digital goods. But why should anyone transfer his hard drive to take advantage of the first sale doctrine. The hard drive did not form part of the transaction and should be kept out. The copyright owner has not invested in the material medium. Even so, Redigi asserts that the same file that is on the user's computer is migrated to the server. Only one file exists, there is no reproduction. The court determined that reproduction means reproducing the file on a new medium, in this case the server. It said there can be no transfer of a digital file as every transfer will implicate the reproduction right of the copyright owner.

Let's say that I am viewing a copyrighted work on my laptop. My act of viewing itself involves reproducing that work. If such acts of reproduction are illegal I may well stop using the internet. In *Mai v. Peak* it was held that loading a computer programme into the RAM of a computer for repair is reproduction within the meaning of the statute. In order to avoid the quagmire, the congress enacted an amendment to Section 117 of the *US copyright act*, which deals with permissible acts of reproduction of a computer programme, to include repair and maintenance. But how far has the situation improved is doubtful. The reproduction rights are only available to owners of a copy of a computer programme. But as the trend is towards licensing and licensees are not owners, the provision has no value. In addition it is only applicable to computer programmes and not to other digital goods. I am confounded as my act of playing a song on my laptop in the US, purchased through iTunes is still infringing the reproduction rights of the copyright holder when it is copied in the RAM of my computer.

A remarkable case which I analogise to transferring in the digital medium is *C.M. Paula Co. v. Logan*.[45] In here Paula contended that by lifting images off its greeting cards and transferring them to ceramic tiles and then selling them, Logan infringed its reproduction and distribution right. The court determined there was no infringement of copyright as the images were lifted in its entirety to the ceramic tiles; no new material object was created. But there is a new material object being created which is the tile with the image. In effect it is the same thing that Redigi asserts. The music is transferred in its entirety to the server. It is strange how an image transferred to the tile does not create a new material object but transferring a song to the server creates a new material object assuming that the same song is transferred in its entirety to the server bit by bit.

---

[45] 355 F. Supp.189, 190 (N.D. Tex. 1973).

Beam me up Scotty said Captain Kirk and the transporter begins to dematerialise Kirk on the spaceship and then reassembles him on a planet ravaged by the mighty dragons. The line referring to the fictional famous transporter of Star Trek, teleports humans atom by atom in such a way that no atom is in two places at the same time. Will this amount to reproducing Kirk? The atoms before and after the teleportation are the same. Which means it is the same Kirk. Is Redigi correct when it argues that the music file is transferred in the same manner? If the transfer is at the atomic level there can be no question of reproduction.

The leading Canadian case of *Théberge v. Galerie d'Art du Petit Champlain Inc.* shines more light on the issue of reproduction.[46] The court found that reproduction involves an increase in the number of copies in existence.[47] In other words, if there is only one copy left in the end it does not amount to reproduction. Accordingly it has to be concluded that the US position with respect to digital transfers is anachronistic. Digital transfers implicate the reproduction rights even though there is only one copy remaining in the end.

The distribution rights are contained in Section 106(3) of the *US copyright act*. It states that the copyright owner has the right to distribute copies or phonorecords of the copyrighted work to the public by sale or other transfer of ownership or by rental, lease or lending. The first sale doctrine is contained in section 109(a) of the act. I have mentioned in 2.3.2, in the last paragraph, that reproduction and distribution rights are literally limited to material objects in the US. But the courts have extended it by a long stretch of imagination to digital goods. This means that the first sale doctrine should by the same stretch of imagination be extended to digital goods. Peer to peer file sharing had been popular a while back such as Napster.[48] But in the file sharing platform Napster was only an intermediary. With application software it helped connect computers to each other which facilitated the exchange of music. Napster itself did not provide content. The problem lies not in distribution. A person could transfer his legally purchased online music so long as he transfers the exact copy that he paid for. He should also not retain a copy when file sharing. But who is going to check whether a person has retained a file or not. It will be very difficult to monitor such actions in the online world. But the same can be said for the physical world. When lending a book I can photocopy the pages and it will be equally difficult to monitor as in the online world. Therefore the problem still remains, even though the act of making a copy is the main issue with digital goods according to the copyright owners. If technological advances could replicate the transfer of

---

[46] [2002] 2 SCR 336 [Théberge].
[47] Paul Torremans, Copyright law: A handbook of contemporary research (Edward Elgar, UK 2007) 64.
[48] 239 F.3d 1004 (9th Cir. 2001).

tangible goods in the digital domain then there should not be a problem in taking advantage of the first sale doctrine for digital goods including software.

However at the moment there is no digital first sale doctrine in the US. Digital goods cannot be alienated including resale. As the argument about digital first sale doctrine is in its infancy and with technology being born everyday this stand of the US should not hold very long.

4.3 Licensing of bits and bytes

The issue of licensing is important as it excludes the application of the first sale doctrine/rule of exhaustion. As the rule of exhaustion/doctrine of first sale applies only to goods which have been sold and not licensed, digital goods which are usually licensed fall outside the ambit of the doctrine. Copyright licensing involves rights owners, rights managers, rights users and end users across the different media types.[49] It is a mechanism used by right-holders to authorize others to use their intellectual property under agreed terms and conditions.[50] However in this portion of the paper we will confine our discussion to the end user licensing agreements (EULA).

Let us talk about the subject matters of copyright which has been fixed in a material medium such as a newspaper or a video home system (VHS) tape of Victor Fleming's, 'Gone with the Wind'. If I pay for a purchase I pay for keeps. It is called a sale. When you sell something there is undoubtedly a transfer of ownership in the property. And you cannot own something if you do not possess it. Possession is considered 9/10th of ownership in law, in other words, a prima facie evidence of ownership.

In order to understand what a license is, firstly, we will examine how sale applies to physical goods which are tangible. Section 202 of the *US copyright act* states that copyright work is distinct from the material medium in which it is fixed. So when I buy a VHS tape of Gone with the Wind, I have paid for the magnetised reel and the plastic cover that protects it from damage. But have I actually paid for the copyright work? In a sense I have. I wouldn't pay for a VHS tape if it had nothing in it. I have paid in order to see the brilliance of Clark Cable and of course to enjoy the picture as a whole. But I cannot modify or edit the picture or even make copies for commercial purposes. The reason for this is because I have not bought any of the rights to the picture. That is still owned by the copyright owner. I have merely paid to watch a copy of the picture. So essentially the real picture is different from the material medium in

---

[49] Is copyright licensing fit for purpose for the digital age? Available at : http://www.ipo.gov.uk/dce-report-phase1.pdf
[50] WIPO global meeting on emerging copyright licensing modalities, Available at :
http://www.wipo.int/meetings/en/2010/wipo_cr_lic_ge_10/

which a copy is embodied. But as I have paid a substantial amount of money, not substantial in comparison to the cost in making the picture, I still have certain rights to the copy. I can invite my friends for a movie night and watch the picture or even give it away to my sister who lives a thousand miles away from me. The ability to do all those things signifies ownership. On the contrary, buying the picture is a lot different from buying the material medium in which a copy of it is embodied. Aside from being financially very sound in order for me to pay for the real picture, I then own the rights to the picture. I can then dictate the terms and conditions of its use.

Buying digital goods can be analogised to buying tangible physical goods. I don't see much of a difference except for the issue of fixation of the copyright work. By now we have understood fixation in terms of tangible physical goods and that digital goods are intangible in nature. If digital goods are intangible so is speech. But that digital goods are intangible is a right statement, I am not sure. Intellectual property in general is intangible when it is in the form of an idea. It becomes tangible only when expressed in some material form. So it will be wrong to assume that digital goods are unexpressed. It is expressed in some material form that is why we are able to read an e-book downloaded on a reader. But where exactly are digital goods fixed? I can say it is fixed on the monitor from where my eyes are able to perceive the individual letters that make up the sentence. Then again you could ask the question, how did it come on the monitor? As mentioned, digital goods are information in bits and bytes, which means those bits and bytes have somehow travelled through the internet network into your reader and stored in its memory. So it is the memory in which the digital goods are fixed. But that is also not a very accurate picture. The computer while deciphering those bits and bytes has to read that information before it is displayed onto the monitor. While reading, it makes a copy, in the temporary memory. This means there is a permanent memory and a temporary memory. But from where did the bits and bytes come into your reader in the first place? I am not a technology specialist so I won't go deep into the matter in case I get it wrong. Those bits and bytes, which are pieces of information, travel in packets through the internet network from one of the servers located around the world where it is ultimately stored. Which means the same digital good can be at many places at the same time. But I will not pay for a bunch of zeroes and ones. It is only when it is displayed on the monitor that it has any value or makes sense. But digital goods are fixed, or at least stored, in the modern sense of the word, in a physical medium such as a hard drive, removable media or server which is comparable to a tangible book where alphabets are stored in its pages.

Then why apply sale to tangible goods and license to digital goods? Among digital goods software is almost always licensed, therefore, we will refer to software licenses and analogise that to digital goods in general. But what exactly is a license? Can a license to use the goods for perpetuity amount to a sale? In lay man's term license is a kind of a sale accompanied by an agreement that restricts the user's rights in law to a copyright product.

On my personal computer I have installed Microsoft security essentials to monitor viruses and malwares. Let me take a look at the license agreement. It states that this agreement is between Microsoft Corporation and me, the user. It adds, it applies to the software, and includes the media on which I received it. As I have downloaded the software and not purchased it on a CD-ROM, the media can only mean my permanent storage, which is my hard drive. Now my hard drive is encumbered by the agreement. But it does not only contain the Microsoft software but other copyright digital goods as well. How fair is it for Microsoft to burden my hard drive with legal obligations even though the software is fixed in only a tiny portion of it. The agreement is a standard form of a contract as it states that by using the software you agree to the terms and conditions of the agreement and that if you are not comfortable with the terms do not use the software. Even the slightest opportunity to negotiate is unavailable. Either I take it or leave it. Under the clause 'scope of the license' it specifically states that the software is "not sold" but licensed. It only gives me some of the rights to use the software. Some of the restrictions listed are, publish the software for others to copy, reverse engineer or decompile, rent or lease the software and transfer the software. Another interesting issue is the clause regarding applicable law. It states that the laws applicable will be the laws of the state where you acquired the software. Let's say I downloaded the software in Norway. But the server from where I downloaded it is located in the US. Which will be the state where I acquired the software? It won't be wrong to say that I acquired the software in the US but I received it in Norway which in the virtual world is the right view. Therefore, the importance of a license lies in the fact that it restricts post sale use and affects the applicable law.

In the US the position is more favourable towards licensing rather than sale. It should be noted that the three cases referred to below deal with tangible copies of software and not intangible copies. First in the line of cases is *Softman Products Co. v. Adobe Systems Inc.*[51] In this case Softman, a software distributor company, unbundled Adobe's software and sold it individually to its customers. Adobe contended that by selling individual pieces and not the bundle as a whole Softman was liable for infringement of copyright and the terms of its

---

[51] 171 F. Supp. 2d 1075 (C.D. Cal. 2001).

license. The court ruled that the transaction was a sale and not a license. There was no privity of contract between Adobe and Softman and that the shrink wrap license (EULA) did not apply to Softman as it did not load the software. As such Softman had the right to resell the software individually under the first sale doctrine.

The second US case is *Vernor v. Autodesk* [52] in which the court found that the customer of the computer software was a licensee and not the owner and thus was not entitled to invoke the first sale doctrine. In this case the court found that if three conditions are met it is a license and not a sale. They are (a) it specifies that the user is granted a licence, (b) significantly restrict the user's ability to transfer the software and (c) imposes notable use restrictions. According to this guideline my Microsoft security essentials is a license and I don't enjoy the right under the first sale doctrine as I am not the owner.

Supposing a license imposes notable use restrictions but on the other hand they are permissible under the *US copyright law*. Which will prevail, the license agreement or the provisions of the statute? Section 117 of the *US copyright act* authorises certain uses of a computer programme such as making a copy in the utilisation of a computer programme or in its maintenance or repair. But the right is only limited to the owner of a computer programme. So in essence, the license will always prevail over the statute as the licensees will not be covered by the beneficial provisions of the statute.

Another interesting US case is *UMG Recordings, Inc. v. Augusto*. [53] In here, the 9th circuit as in Vernor v. Autodesk held that the first sale doctrine applies not only when a copy is first sold but also when a copy is given away or the title is otherwise transferred. What will amount to a transfer of title? Other than sale, to me, parting with a good with the intention of not having anything to do with it will amount to a transfer of title. The intention is paramount. Even the slightest of reserved intention will annul the transfer of title. A transfer of title happens when I gift a stranger my book. But if I dictate terms like on which days he is to read the pages and that he should leave the last five pages and return the book at the end of the 7th day, it clearly shows that I didn't have the intention of transferring title. This I would call a license to read rather than a transfer of title.

Even for software distributed online by means of download, the case of *MDY v Blizzard* tells us that the licence view is more favourable. [54] In this case, the US court of appeal for the ninth

---

[52] 621 F.3d 1102, (9th Cir. 2010).
[53] 628 F.3d 1175, (9th Cir. 2011).
[54] 629 F.3d 928 (9th Cir. 2010).

circuit held that online software should be considered licensed and not sold. Thus, in the US as long as the requirements in Vernor v. Autodesk are met, the license view takes precedence over sale irrespective of the medium in which the software is fixed.

In the EU, the position with regards to software has been discussed in the UsedSoft case. As long as the licence involves a onetime fee and allows the user to use the software for an unlimited period in time, it is a sale and therefore the rule of exhaustion is applicable.

5. The future

5.1 What next?

Have we reached the pinnacle of technological progress or is it just the beginning? Technology has progressed side by side with the evolution of mankind, and it will keep on evolving as we evolve. We started by painting on rocks and writing on wood, and now we have come so far where we fix ideas on mediums where they are imperceptible, unless aided with the help of computers.

If the main culprit for the exclusion of the first sale doctrine/rule of exhaustion in reselling digital goods is that it necessarily involves copying when transferring, then cloud computing is an answer. In the simplest terms, cloud computing means storing, sharing and accessing data, which could include your digital copyright works, over the internet instead of your computer's hard drive.[55] So the whole idea of transferring your digital copyright work takes a backseat. A cloud locker can be used for file sharing with anyone. All you need to do is create links for the files you want to share and send it to the recipients. The recipients then need to click on the links which gives them access to the files. In this way there is no transfer of the copyright material so the questions of infringement of the reproduction rights do not arise. It is like sharing a book with your friend. Reproduction rights will only be implicated if someone downloaded the files from the cloud locker to his hard drive or any other removable storage device.

Amazon has patented a used digital marketplace and its outcome is dependent on the Redigi case.[56] On January 29, 2014 Redigi announced that it was awarded a patent for its technology to migrate music files without making a copy.[57] Is second hand market for digital goods the future? If Redigi has been granted a patent for the ability to move files without making a copy then there can be no objection to the application of the first sale doctrine/rule of exhaustion to digital goods, at least in the US. If there was an objection it would not have been granted a patent in the first place. The whole argument of the people opposed to the digital first sale doctrine, was that the copy that you transfer is not the original copy that you paid for. But now that such a technology exists where you can transfer the original copy that you paid for without retaining a copy, the oppositions argument crumbles. However in the EU problems would still creep up. This is because distribution of digital copyright works, with the

[55] Available at : http://www.pcmag.com/article2/0,2817,2372163,00.asp
[56] Available at : http://newsroom.redigi.com/redigi-issues-statement-on-amazons-patent-for-the-resale-of-used-digital-goods/
[57] Available at : http://newsroom.redigi.com/redigi-inc-awarded-significant-u-s-patent/

exception of computer programmes, fall under the communication to the public right or making available to the public right, for which, according to the *Infosoc directive* the rule of exhaustion does not apply. Unlike the US where the first sale doctrine does not apply to digital goods because a transfer implicates the reproduction rights of the copyright owner, in the EU the *Infosoc directive* itself restricts the rule of exhaustion to tangible physical goods irrespective of whether a transfer of digital goods implicates the reproduction right of the copyright owner or not. For it to apply in the EU there will have to be an amendment to Article 3 of the *Infosoc directive*.

In the future the transient nature of digital goods will be even more notable. Streaming instead of downloading a copyright work is already gaining popularity. Devices like personal computers could be completely obliterated. I cannot wait to imagine a day when man and machine will become one. This prediction is already in the making in the shape of google glass. Google glass is a wearable electronic device which lets you access information. The glass explorer edition terms of service states that "you may not resell, loan, transfer, or give your device to any other person. If you resell, loan, transfer, or give your device to any other person without Google's authorization, Google reserves the right to deactivate the device, and neither you nor the unauthorized person using the device will be entitled to any refund, product support, or product warranty."[58]

Hail to the new world, where companies retain control of not only digital goods like software and entertainment media, but also your electronic devices, even after consumers have purchased them.

---

[58] See device specific addendum, Available at: http://www.google.com/glass/termsofuse/

6. Conclusion

In this work, I have tried to discuss the issues in the resale of digital goods. I started by discussing the basics of copyright law, which are applicable not only to tangible goods but also to intangible digital goods, such as, the subject matter of copyright, the fixation of copyright works and the reproduction and distribution rights. Also discussed, was the rule of exhaustion/doctrine of first sale, which is an exception to the distribution rights of the copyright owner, and which allows a buyer of a copyright work to alienate his copy of the work.

It was because of the nature in transferring digital goods, which is not the same as transferring tangible goods, that a buyer of an intangible digital good is unable to alienate his copy of the work once he has paid for it. Every transfer in the digital medium involves making a new copy, which in turn infringes the reproduction rights of the copyright owner. The trend of licensing of digital goods was another reason why it is not possible to resell your legally purchased digital copy of a copyright work. As a result, the buyer of a digital copyright work is unable to take advantage of the first sale doctrine/rule of exhaustion.

As discussed in the introduction, copyright laws grow obsolete as new technological advances take place. No matter how neutral the wordings of the statute, at some point in time the language of the statute is unable to accommodate the advances in technology. This is a time when those who have a stake in the legislation get a chance to draft it according to their own whims and fancies in their personal interest, with some of their concerns being legitimate. They argued that it is easy to replicate and distribute digital goods, so the doctrine of first sale/rule of exhaustion should not apply to digital goods. They were successful in convincing the lawmakers, who in turn drafted the legislation in their favour at the cost of the general public. The result was that the doctrine of first sale/rule of exhaustion became inapplicable to digital goods.

But the arguments put forward by the people who have a stake in the legislation are somewhat sketchy. The Berne three-step test, in Article 9 (2) of the BC, delicately balances the public and the private interests. The dual goal of copyright law is to ensure that a creator of a work is rewarded amply for his intellectual creation and at the same time the public is able to enjoy the art and literature that the society has to offer. The Berne three-step test does this by setting limits to the reproduction right of the copyright owners, allowing limitations in certain special cases that do not conflict with the normal exploitation of the work and that do not unreasonably prejudice the legitimate interests of the authors. Although the Berne three-step test is limited to the reproduction right of the copyright owners, other international instruments, such as the *TRIPS* agreement, has incorporated it in Article 13. Under the *TRIPS* agreement, it applies to all the exclusive rights of the copyright owner and is not just limited to reproduction rights.

What I am trying to say is, if a certain action, such as reselling your digital copy of a copyright work, which has been legally and lawfully acquired, allows the copyright owner to normally exploit his work without prejudicing his legitimate interest, then the liberty granted to the public, such as the right to alienate his copy of the copyright work, based on the first sale doctrine/rule of exhaustion, should not be abrogated.

Patents being given for technology to migrate digital files without making a copy, goes on to show the dynamic nature of technological advances. If we for a moment assume that technological progress should come in the way of public interest, then by the end of the 21st century, copyright owners will have absolute monopoly in the way they exploit their intellectual creations. There will be a decline in the culture, science and innovation as fewer people are able to enjoy works of art and literature, due to restrictions placed on the access to copyright works.

The benefit to the public aspect of copyright law should stay intact, and just because the way we consume copyright works has changed in the digital age, it should afford no excuse to abrogate the limits placed on the exclusive rights of the copyright owners. The doctrine of first sale has been a part of copyright law since it was codified in the *US copyright act* of 1909. The benefits of having a limitation on the distribution rights of the copyright owners are no secret.

Having a digital first sale doctrine will result in a secondary market for digital goods. In the EU, a flourishing market for used software has spawned from the judgement in the UsedSoft case. There is little reason not to extend it to other digital copyright goods. The divide, with respect to the resale of digital goods between the US and the EU is also worrying. The US does not differentiate between software and other digital goods. Software and other digital goods are not eligible for resale in the US, unlike in the EU, where software is eligible for resale, but not other digital goods. Such practices only create uncertainties in copyright law. It also divides the market which is an obstacle in the development of a global digital marketplace.

The way forward, keeping in mind the technological advances, the purpose of copyright law and the delicate balance between the public and private interests that it tries to achieve, will be to extend the doctrines in question to digital goods, for the present copyright laws are out of sync with reality.

References

List of Judgements/Decisions

American Judgements:

A&M Records, Inc. v. Napster, Inc., 239 F.3d 1004 (9th Cir. 2001)

Bobbs Merrill Co. v. Straus, 210 U.S. 339 (Supreme Court 1908)

Capitol Records, Inc. v. Thomas, 579 F. Supp. 2d 1210, 1225 (D. Minn. 2008)

C. M. Paula Co. v. Logan, 355 F. Supp.189, 190 (N.D. Tex. 1973)

Capitol Records, LLC v. Redigi Inc., 934 F.Supp.2d 640 (S.D.N.Y. 2013)

Harrison v. Maynard, Merrill and Co., 61 F. 689 (C.C.A, Second Circuit 1894)

Mai Systems Corp. v. Peak Computer, Inc., 991 F.2d 511 (9th Cir. 1993)

MDY Industries v. Blizzard Entertainment Inc., 629 F.3d 928 (9th Cir. 2011)

Softman Products Company LLC v. Adobe Systems Inc., 171 F. Supp. 2d 1075 (C.D. Cal. 2001)

UMG Recordings Inc. v. Augusto, 628 F.3d 1175 (9th Cir. 2011)

Vernor v. Autodesk Inc., 621 F.3d 1102 (9th Cir. 2010)

European Judgements:

Case C-466/12 *Nils Svensson and Others v. Retriever Sverige AB* [2014]

Case C-128/11 *UsedSoft GmbH v. Oracle International Corporation* [2012] 3 C.M.L.R. 44

Case 78/70 *Deutsche Grammophon GmbH v. Metro-SB-Grossmarkte GmbH & Co. KG* [1971] ECR 487, [1971] CMLR 631

T.G.I Paris, 11th December 1985, Dalloz 1987, somm. p. 155, note Colombet Claude

Canadian Judgement:

Théberge v. Galerie d'Art du Petit Champlain Inc. [2002] 2 SCR 336 [Théberge]

Treaties/Statutes

International treaties and conventions:

Berne Convention for the Protection of Literary and Artistic Works, as amended in 1976

WIPO Copyright Treaty, 1996

TRIPS Agreement, 1994

European Legislations:

Directive 2001/29/EC on the harmonisation of certain aspects of copyright and related rights in the information society

Directive 2009/24/EC on the legal protection of computer programmes

Directive 96/9/EC on the legal protection of databases

American legislation:

US Copyright Act, 1976 (Title 17 of the United States Code)

Secondary Literature

Books:

Copyright: Sacred text, Technology, and the DMCA, Nimmer, David (Kluwer Law International) 2003

Copyright law: A handbook of contemporary research, Torremans, Paul (Edward Elgar) 2007

Copyright in the Information Society, Shapiro, Ted & Lindner, Brigitte (Edward Elgar) 2011

Contemporary Intellectual Property, 2nd ed., MacQueen, Hector, et al. (Oxford University Press) 2011

Digital Copyright, Litman, Jessica (Prometheus books) 2001

Law, Economics and Cyberspace, Salzberger, M., Eli & Elkin-Koren, Niva (Edward Elgar) 2004

Research Handbook on the Future of EU Copyright, Derclaye, Estelle (Edward Elgar) 2009

Technology and copyright law, Cheeseman, Lawrence & Bielefield, Arlene (Neal-Schuman Publishers) 1997

Articles:

Choderker, Ivy, *The First Sale Doctrine defence as a limit on the right of publicity: Allison v. Vintage Sports Plaques*, 19 Loy L.A. Entertainment L. Rev. 413, 422 (1999).

Calaba, Victor F., *Quibbles 'n Bits: Making A Digital First Sale Doctrine Feasible*, 9 Mich. Telecomm. Tech. L. Rev. 1 (2002)

Geist, Rachel Ann, *A License to Read: The Effect of e-books on Publishers, Libraries and the First Sale Doctrine*, 52 Idea 63, (2012)

Loebbecke, C., *Digital goods: An economic perspective*, Encyclopaedia of Information Systems, Volume 1, 635, (Elsevier Inc.) 2002

Lichtman, Douglas, *Copyright as a rule of evidence*, 52 Duke L.J. 683, (2003)

Quah, Danny, *Digital Goods and the New Economy* (2002), Available at: http://econ.lse.ac.uk/staff/dquah/p/dp-0212hbne.pdf

Reports:

Association littéraire et artistique international, *Report on the making available and communication to the public in the internet environment*, Available at: http://www.alai.org/assets/files/resolutions/making-available-right-report-opinion.pdf

Is copyright licensing fit for purpose for the digital age? Available at: http://www.ipo.gov.uk/dce-report-phase1.pdf

WIPO global meeting on emerging copyright licensing modalities, Available at: http://www.wipo.int/meetings/en/2010/wipo_cr_lic_ge_10/